AIRBUS A320
ROBBIE SHAW

First published in the UK in 1996
by Airlife Publishing Ltd.

British Library Cataloguing in Publication Data available

A catalogue record for this book is available from the British Library

ISBN 1 85310 568 6

Typeset by Litho Link Ltd, Welshpool, Powys, Wales
Printed in Hong Kong

Airlife Publishing Ltd

101 Longden Road, Shrewsbury SY3 9EB, England

Introduction

However optimistic they may have been when the Airbus project first began back in 1965, I'm sure the directors of the company could not have foreseen that thirty years later Airbus would take more orders in a single year than that great plane maker Boeing. (During 1994 orders placed for Airbus Industrie aircraft exceeded those of Boeing by one.)

Airbus Industrie was set up in December 1970 to manage the development, manufacture, marketing and support of the twin engined A300 medium-haul wide-bodied airliner; the prime contractors were Aerospatiale, Deutsche Airbus and Hawker-Siddeley (later British Aerospace). These were later joined by CASA of Spain. Components manufactured by these companies are transported to the assembly line at Toulouse, where all flight testing and pre-delivery work is undertaken prior to the aircraft being handed over to the customer. The first A300 took to the air at Toulouse on its maiden flight on 28 October 1978, with the smaller A310 following in April 1982.

To complement its wide-bodied types, Airbus decided to expand its family and offer a smaller short-medium-range single-aisle twin-engined aircraft to compete with the larger 737 variants Boeing was planning. This was the A320. The aircraft was to offer seating capacity in the range of 150 to 180 passengers in a spacious cabin with 3×3 seating, which can be reduced to 2×2 in first/business class. Airbus took the opportunity to make optimum use of advanced design concepts, new materials and advanced avionics for its new creation. Apart from the leading edge of the fin, the entire tail fin and tailplane are fabricated from carbon-fibre reinforced plastics. It is also the first subsonic commercial aircraft to feature fly by wire (FBW) control systems, and the first to feature revolutionary side-stick controllers in place of the standard control column or yoke. These features are now standard on subsequent additions to the Airbus range – the A319, A321, A330 and A340 – enabling pilots to have common type ratings.

The FBW system features five main computers which operate, via hydraulic jacks, all primary and secondary flight controls, except for the rudder and tailplane trim. The systems are so advanced that they will not permit the pilot to exceed the aircraft's limitations; this includes the pilot being unable either to stall the aircraft or exceed the 'g' limitations. There has been much discussion in professional publications about these systems employed in the A320; some feel that the pilot is no longer in full control of his aircraft and he is but a servant of the computers. It is true that some crews who have transferred to the aircraft from other types were sceptical, but the crews I have spoken to have nothing but praise for the aircraft and its systems, and most would now prefer to fly the A320 rather than any other type.

Two engine types were offered to prospective customers, the CFM56 and the IAE V2500, though the latter was not available for early deliveries. The letters IAE stand for International Aero Engines, a consortium of five manufacturers: Fiat (Italy), Japanese Aero Engines Corporation, MTU (Germany), Pratt & Whitney (USA) and Rolls-Royce (UK). These manufacturers signed an agreement in March 1983 to develop an advanced technology turbofan engine for future short-medium-haul airliners. The designation V2500 was created simply by using V as the Roman numeral five (the number of manufacturers), and the figures 2500, denoting the 25,000lb thrust. The cowlings and wing pylons for both engines are manufactured from composite materials, and the engines are easily distinguishable due to the differing design of their cowlings.

The aircraft is assembled at the Toulouse factory where Aerospatiale is responsible for manufacture of the forward fuselage, centre wing box and engine pylons. MBB of Germany builds the centre and rear fuselage, tailcone, wing flaps, fin and rudder. British Aerospace builds the wings, ailerons, spoilers and airbrakes, while CASA contributes the tailplane, elevators and mainwheel doors. All large major components are flown to Toulouse inside the Super Guppy transporter operated by Airbus, which will soon be replaced by the specially designed A300 Super Transporter, the 'Beluga'.

Airbus announced on 2 March 1984 that it was to proceed with the A320, the initial variant being the A320-100 series. However, only twenty-one aircraft of this variant were built, as the later series -200 became available in the autumn of 1988. The latter variant features wing centre-section fuel tanks and has an increased maximum take-off weight. The A320-200 also has winglets, which distinguish it externally from the -100 variant. The prototype A320-100 first flew on 22 February 1987, and over the following months was joined by four others, all of which were used in the flight test and certification programme. First delivery was to Air France on 28 March 1988, with British Airways receiving its first aircraft three days later. The latter airline, not exactly renowned for its support of European aircraft, took delivery by default as it inherited an order for ten aircraft with the take-over of British Caledonian. In fact the first two aircraft had already been completed and painted in British Caledonian livery at the time. The British Airways A320 fleet comprises five each of both variants. French carriers Air France and Air Inter are the only other operators of the A320-100, seven of which were delivered to the latter, and have been supplemented by twenty-six -200 variants. Air France took delivery of seven A320-100s, the two remaining aircraft being retained by Airbus, though one was subsequently converted to -200 standard and delivered to the French national carrier.

The maiden flight of the first A320-200 took place on 27 June 1988, and the first V2500-powered machine a month later on 28 July 1988. Adria Airways, of the then Yugoslavia, was the first customer for the V2500-powered version. By 1 June 1989 a total of 472 A320s had been ordered by twenty-five customers, and by the end of 1992 there were 362 A320s in service with thirty-six customers. During 1992 Airbus delivered 111 A320s, a quite amazing feat. One of the first Asian customers was Indian Airlines, and for this customer Airbus has replaced the standard twin-wheel main landing gear with four-wheel bogies to enable the airline to operate the type from low-strength runways.

The A320 has been selling well in almost every corner of the world, but perhaps the most surprising and pleasing aspect for Airbus is the type's penetration into the North American market. In Canada both Air Canada and Canadian Airlines International have large A320 fleets, whilst charter operators Canada 3000 and Skyservice also operate the type. Across the border, Boeing has no doubt been hurt by the selection of the A320 by some of America's major carriers: America West, Braniff, Northwest and United. The latter two operators placed orders for fifty aircraft, and United has options for a further fifty. United operates its A320s in a 144-seat configuration, and the airline is the first customer to power its A320s with the IAE V2527-A5, a derated version of the engine which powers the A321.

To date four A320s have been lost in accidents, providing

ammunition for opponents of the type and its FBW and computer systems. The first accident was to an Air France machine which crashed at Habsheim on 26 June 1988 whilst carrying out a demonstration flight. On 14 February 1990 Indian Airlines lost an aircraft on final approach to Bangalore, and although the aircraft was being flown manually by the crew, the Indian authorities grounded the type for a short period. It should be noted, however, that this action was not repeated by airworthiness authorities anywhere else in the world. Air Inter lost an aircraft on 20 January 1992 which crashed twenty kilometres short of its destination, Strasbourg. The final loss was to a Lufthansa machine on 14 September 1993 which ran off the end of a very wet runway at Warsaw. These losses must not be taken out of context, however, as these statistics are no worse than most types of airliner in service, including the Boeing 737, though it has to be said not as good as the exceptional safety record of the Boeing 757 and 767.

It is inconceivable that sales of the A320 will come anywhere near those of the world's best-selling airliner, the Boeing 737. However, there is no doubt that Airbus have built an exceptional aircraft which is extremely popular with passengers, and United Airlines claims that the A320 is the best new aircraft entry into service they have ever experienced. Airbus figures show that a total of 656 A320s have been ordered to date, over 500 of which have now been delivered. The 500th aircraft, the twenty-second for United, was delivered to the airline on 20 January 1995.

The following airlines have operated the A320, including those who operated the type on lease. Those in brackets no longer do so, or indeed no longer exist.

Adria, (Aero Lloyd), Air Canada, Air Charter, (Air Columbus), Air France, Air Inter, AirLanka, Air Malta, Air Nippon, Air Portugal, Airtours International, Airworld, Air 2000, All Nippon, (Ambassador), America West, Ansett Australia, (Bahamasair), Balkan, (Braniff), British Airways, British Mediterranean, Caledonian, Canada 3000, Canadian Airlines International, China Airlines, (Conair), Cretan Airlines, Cyprus Airways, Dragonair, Egyptair, Eurocypria, Excalibur, (Flitestar), Gulf Air, Holiday Air, Iberia, Indian Airlines, (Inter European Airways), Kuwait Airways, LACSA, Ladeco, (Leisure Air), Lufthansa, Mexicana, Monarch, Northwest, (Oasis), Onur Air, (Pegasus), Premiair, Royal Jordanian, (Ryanair), (Saarland Airlines), SAETA, Shorouk Air, Skyservice, South African Airways, Southeast European Airlines, Sudan Airways, Swissair, (TACA International Airlines), (Trans Alsace), TransAsia, Translift Airways, (Transmed), Tunis Air, United Airlines, (United European Airways), Vietnam Airlines, (WDL Aviation).

Acknowledgements

I would like to thank my friends Paul Hooper and Iain Logan for their invaluable assistance. Unless otherwise credited, all photographs were taken by the author using Kodachrome 64 film.

Robbie Shaw, April 1995

SPECIFICATIONS		
	A320-100	**A320-200**
First flight date	22 February 1987	27 June 1988
Max. accommodation	179	180
Wing span	34.10m (111ft 10in)	34.10m (111ft 10in)
Length	37.57m (123ft 3in)	37.57m (123ft 3in)
Height	11.76m (38ft 7in)	11.76m (38ft 7in)
Max. t/o weight	68,000kg (149,915lb)	77,000kg (166,400lb)
Range with max. pax.	3,240km (1,710nm)	5,280km (2,850nm)
Max. cruising speed	Mach 0.82	Mach 0.82

ADRIA AIRWAYS (JP/ADR)

Slovenia's Adria Airways has suffered significantly in the civil wars of the former Yugoslavia, and has only returned to something resembling normal operations within the last year. The airline was formed in 1961 as Adria Airways, though the name changed to Inex Adria Airways in 1968. The airline operated charter services primarily aimed at ferrying tourists to Yugoslavia. In 1986 the airline returned to its original title Adria Airways and also commenced limited scheduled services. During the first eighteen months of the civil war the airline was forced to cease operations, particularly when a couple of aircraft, including one A320, were damaged by air raids on Brnik airport. During this period most of the fleet operated on behalf of other carriers, such as British Air Ferries, or were leased out. A number of the DC-9/MD-80 fleet have returned to Adria service, though at one time all three A320s were on lease to Cretan Airlines. The simple livery comprises an all-white fuselage with large dark blue titles. On the white tail is the logo of a dark blue and turquoise heart shape lying sideways to form an arrowhead. Photographed in 1991 while still Yugoslavian registered is A320-200 YU-AOA. The ICAO callsign is 'ADRIA'. *(Robbie Shaw)*

AIR CANADA (AC/ACA)

Formed as Trans Canada Airlines in 1937, the airline commenced services between Vancouver and nearby Seattle, with transcontinental services to Toronto the following year. During the 1960s the airline operated British-built equipment, namely the Viscount and Vanguard. In 1965 it changed its name to Air Canada and, in addition to a large network throughout Canada and the USA, the company had a strong presence on transatlantic routes. A fleet of DC-9s acquired from 1967 onwards still soldier on, though the younger Boeing 727s have been replaced by thirty-four A320s, with a further sixteen on option. The company has also recently taken delivery of Canadair Regional Jets for some cross-border and domestic services, whilst Boeing 767s are used for transcontinental and international services in support of 747 Jumbos. Air Canada's new livery was unveiled in early 1994, prior to which the colour scheme had remained virtually unchanged for many years. A red cheatline ran the length of the fuselage separating the grey belly from the white cabin, though in recent years a second band in a darker shade of red had been added below the cheatline. The company's logo of a white maple leaf within a circle was prominent on the red fin. Illustrated at Toronto is A320-200 C-FKPS.
(Robbie Shaw)

The new Air Canada livery introduced early in 1994 is based on an all-white fuselage with red titling with a large red maple leaf on a dark green fin, though it has to be said the dark green appears more like black. The first A320 to appear in the new livery was C-FDSU, seen here climbing out after take-off from runway 24R at Toronto's Lester B. Pearson airport. The ICAO callsign is 'AIR CANADA'. *(Robbie Shaw)*

AIR CHARTER (SF/ACF)

Formed in 1966 Air Charter is a subsidiary of Air France and has regularly operated aircraft types leased from the parent company. As the name suggests, Air Charter operates inclusive and ad hoc charters, and sometimes operates flights on behalf of the parent company. The first jet equipment used was the Sud-Aviation Caravelle, and presently both Airbus and Boeing types are utilised. Two A300s and two A320s are leased from Air France, while Boeing 727s and 737s, most of which are on lease from another French charter airline Euralair, are also in use. The simple company livery features a white fuselage with red titling on the cabin roof, behind which are blue and red stripes which proceed rearwards and cover half of the fin in a 'streamer' effect. The ICAO callsign is 'AIR CHARTER'. Illustrated is A320-200 F-GLGE. *(Robbie Shaw)*

AIR FRANCE (AF/AFR)

Air France is struggling with heavy losses and disputes with employees. Despite protests of unfair competition, in 1994 the EEC approved a massive injection of French government aid far in excess of the mounting losses; it was hardly surprising that numerous European airlines vociferously opposed this decision. The French national carrier has taken over UTA, and looks set to subsume subsidiary Air Inter, thereby virtually eliminating domestic competition at a stroke. Smaller carriers such as Air Liberté and AOM are trying hard to gain a foothold in the domestic and international network as they too voice their dissent over the aid package. Air France was a launch customer for the A320 and took delivery of the first on 28 March 1988. It presently has twenty-six of the type in use, six of which are A320-100 series aircraft. The airline has leased out nine A320s, two to Air Charter and seven to Vietnam Airlines. Other aircraft in the large inventory include Boeing 737s, 747s and 767s, Airbus A300s, A310s and A340s, and of course Concorde. The Air France livery features an all-white fuselage with blue titling, whilst the tail is encompassed with blue, white and red tricolour stripes in varying widths. Photographed at Heathrow as if taxiing in formation with a Lufthansa aircraft is A320-100 F-GFKG *Ville d'Amsterdam*. The ICAO callsign is 'AIR FRANCE'.
(Robbie Shaw)

AIR INTER (IT/ITF)

A member of the Air France Group, Air Inter's future is currently in doubt. With the take-over of independent airline UTA in 1990 Air France indirectly acquired a share in Air Inter, the country's main domestic carrier which was formed in 1954. Over the past few years Air Inter has also operated a number of European services, some on behalf of its parent airline. Two major decisions taken during 1994, however, now threaten Air Inter. The European Union's decision to force the French government to open Paris's Orly airport to competition has seen airlines such as Air Liberté, AOM and TAT competing on the lucrative routes to Marseilles and Toulouse, ending Air Inter's unfair dominance on these routes. The quite ridiculous amount of state aid being used to bale out the incompetent Air France brought with it some restrictions. Air France is now reportedly looking at setting up a new European carrier in which Air Inter is likely to lose its identity. The colour scheme has a white fuselage with blue and red titling. The rear of the fuselage is light blue which sweeps up to encompass the lower half of the fin, and is separated from the white upper half of the fin by two pennants, one dark blue and one red. Air Inter has thirty-four A320s, six of which are -100 series aircraft, including F-GGEE seen here on approach to Orly. The ICAO callsign is 'AIR INTER'.

(Robbie Shaw)

AIRLANKA (UL/ALK)

AirLanka was formed on 10 January 1979 to succeed the previous national carrier, Air Ceylon. From its base at Colombo the airline has an extensive route network from Asia to Europe, with destinations ranging from Hong Kong to London. Workhorse of the fleet is the Lockheed L1011 Tristar, the first of which was acquired in 1981. Until recently the company had six Tristars on its inventory, though with the recent delivery of two of the three Airbus A340s on order two of the Tristars have been disposed of. The airline also used to operate the Boeing 747, but this type is no longer used.

Domestic services used to be operated by Boeing 737-200s, but have since been replaced by two Airbus A320s, the first being delivered in December 1992. The airline's livery features a white fuselage bisected by a red cheatline which, as it nears the tailplane, broadens to encompass the extreme rear fuselage and tail. The company's large stylised white peacock logo is prominent on the red fin. Black titling and the national flag appear on the cabin roof. Illustrated is the company's first A320-200 4R-ABA. The ICAO callsign is 'AIRLANKA'. *(Airbus Industrie)*

AIR MALTA (KM/AMC)

The national carrier of this small island nation was formed in 1973 and commenced services with leased Tridents while elderly Boeing 720s were acquired the following year. The first Boeing 737-200 was delivered to the airline in 1983, followed by series -300s ten years later. The 737-200s are now being disposed of as the airline takes delivery of five British Aerospace RJ70 Regional Jets. The Airbus fleet comprises two A320s which were acquired in 1990 and 1992, and are now supplemented by a leased A310 which was acquired in time for the 1994 summer season. The current Air Malta livery has a white fuselage with red titling and three thin black stripes on the lower forward fuselage. Most of the fin is red with a large white Maltese cross, while the lower fin is painted white with three black stripes. Photographed inbound to London/Heathrow in December 1992 is the airline's first A320-200 9H-ABP. The ICAO callsign is 'AIR MALTA'. *(Robbie Shaw)*

AIR NIPPON (EL/ANK)

With its base at Tokyo's Haneda domestic airport, Air Nippon is a subsidiary of All Nippon Airways. The airline was formerly known as Nihon Kinkyori Airways and operates regional services with a sizeable fleet of NAMC YS-11s and Boeing 737-200s, the latter being handed down from the parent company. The airline has seven 737-500s on order for 1995/96 delivery, and also utilises a few A320-200s leased from All Nippon. The livery is identical to that of All Nippon, except for the fuselage titling and initials on the fin. The ICAO callsign is 'ANK AIR'. *(Shinya Hata)*

AIR PORTUGAL (TP/TAP)

Now operating under the name Air Portugal, the Portuguese national carrier was until 1979 known as TAP – Transportes Aereos Portugueses. The airline has an extensive network throughout Europe and Africa, as well as across the Atlantic to both North and South America. On European routes A320s and Boeing 737s are used, supplemented by A310s on higher density routes such as London. The A310s are also used on African and some North American services. Long-haul routes are operated by seven Lockheed L1011 Tristars, though these are likely to be disposed of as the first of four A340s has now entered service. The livery features a white upper and grey lower fuselage separated by a thick green and red cheatline which continues halfway up the fin where the initials TAP run vertically in red. The Air Portugal titling is in black on the upper fuselage, forward of which is the national flag. Photographed at Heathrow is CS-TND *Garcia de Orta*, one of six A320-200s on the inventory. The ICAO callsign is 'AIR PORTUGAL'. *(Robbie Shaw)*

AIRTOURS INTERNATIONAL (VZ/AIH)

Manchester-based Airtours International is now a well established UK charter operator, its position strengthened by the take-over of Aspro Holidays and its associate Inter European Airways. With the acquisition of the latter came a fleet of two Airbus A320s and two Boeing 757s, the accompanying Boeing 737s being disposed of. These types operate alongside eight McDonnell Douglas MD-83s to destinations throughout the Mediterranean and the Canary Islands from major bases at Manchester and Gatwick, whilst in the winter additional destinations include airports in Austria and Switzerland for the ski season. The A320s generally operate from regional airports such as Bristol and Cardiff. Rumour has it the airline would like to dispose of its MD-83s and acquire further A320s. In the meantime four aged ex-Eastern Airlines 757s have just been acquired after years of storage in the desert. The former Inter European Boeing 757s currently operate alongside two Boeing 767-300ERs in the long-haul division which was set up in the spring of 1994 primarily to operate services to Florida. In 1993 Airtours failed in a bid to take over rival Owners Abroad and its airline Air 2000. The Airtours livery has white fuselage with dark blue titles below the window line forward of the wing root. The belly is deep blue and sweeps up to encompass the rear fuselage and fin, and is trimmed by turquoise pinstripes. In the centre of the fin is the company logo of a rearwards-facing deep blue 'A' trimmed in turquoise on a royal blue disc. The engine nacelles are also deep blue. Photographed at Salzburg in January 1994 is A320-200 G-YJBM. The ICAO callsign is 'KESTREL'. *(Robbie Shaw)*

To show its affinity with the Going Places travel agent chain, Airtours has adopted a slightly revised livery to include the progressive Going Places logo on the fin of its aircraft. In January 1995 the new logo was painted on the company's A320s and Boeing 757s. Photographed at Lanzarote sporting the new tail logo is A320-200 G-SUEE. (Alec Molton)

AIRWORLD (AWD)

One of Britain's newest airlines is Airworld, which was formed early in 1994. Like many holiday charter airlines the airline was founded as a division of a holiday company, in this case Iberotravel Limited which, as the name suggests, concentrates on holidays and package tours to the Iberian peninsula. Although it has its headquarters in London the airline operates primarily from Cardiff and Manchester with a pair of A320-200s, both of which were acquired in May 1994. The airline's colour scheme features an all-white fuselage, apart from a thin orange pinstripe above the window line and dark blue titles. The tail fin and engine nacelles are dark blue upon which is the company's orange stylised globe logo. Illustrated is A320-200 G-BVJW. The ICAO callsign is 'ENVOY'.

AIR 2000 (DP/AMM)

Formed at Manchester in 1987 Air 2000 operates charter flights throughout Europe and to Mexico and North America, and has recently inaugurated scheduled flights to Cyprus. The airline is a subsidiary of First Choice Holidays, previously known as Owner's Abroad. The airline has a justified reputation of excellence, and provides an in-flight service many a large scheduled carrier would be proud of. From a modest start of two Boeing 757s, the company has steadily expanded and now boasts a modern fleet of fifteen of the Boeing twin-jets, which are supported by four Airbus A320-200s delivered during 1992. Although Manchester-based the airline has a major operating base at Gatwick where six aircraft are based, with another base in Glasgow. The livery features an all-white fuselage with two pinstripe cheatlines in red and gold running below the window line then flaring to encompass the base of the fin. Red Air 2000 titles edged in gold appear on the fin and forward fuselage, whilst the engine cowlings are all red apart from a white mid-band containing a repeat of the fuselage cheatlines. Illustrated soon after delivery in May 1992 is the airline's first A320 G-OOAA. The ICAO callsign is 'JETSET'. *(Robbie Shaw)*

ALL NIPPON AIRWAYS (NH/ANA)

Since its foundation in 1952 All Nippon Airways has gradually expanded and is now Japan's largest carrier. The airline was formed under the name Japan Helicopter and Aeroplane Transport Company and, over the next fifteen years, absorbed four other domestic carriers. Until 1986 All Nippon was not permitted to operate international services and compete with the national carrier, Japan Airlines. Since that date, however, the airline has steadily expanded its network to include destinations in Asia, Europe and North America. On the domestic routes the Boeing 737s have been replaced by A320-200s, seventeen of which have been delivered with a further five on order. These are supplemented by a large fleet of Boeing 767s and 747s. To cater for its future needs the airline has placed orders for the Airbus A340 and Boeing 777, and more recently the A321. The attractive livery has two bands of dark and light blue sweeping diagonally up the fuselage from the nose to encompass the fin, all of which, except the trailing edge, is dark blue with the letters ANA diagonally in white. The belly is light grey and the remainder of the fuselage white, upon which is the airline titling which, for aircraft used only on domestic services, is in Japanese characters only. Illustrated is JA8382. The ICAO callsign is 'ALL NIPPON'. *(Airbus Industrie)*

AMERICA WEST AIRLINES (HP/AWE)

Based in Phoenix, Arizona, America West Airlines has an extensive network throughout the western United States with hubs at Las Vegas and Reno, whilst expansion eastwards has seen the creation of a further hub at Columbus, Ohio. The airline was formed in 1981 as a low-cost domestic operator but has since introduced an international service to Mexico City. Financial problems forced the airline to seek Chapter 11 bankruptcy protection in June 1991, a state it emerged from during 1994. The current fleet comprises over fifty Boeing 737s, the bulk of which are series -300s with a batch of fourteen -400s in the process of delivery. These are supported by seventeen A320s with seven more to follow, and eleven Boeing 757s.

The airline's livery comprises a white fuselage bisected by three blue pinstripes below the window line, with America West titling and logo on the upper fuselage in a shade of burgundy. The white tail features the company stylised 'AW' logo represented as a burgundy sun rising behind silver mountains. America West's A320s are leased from Guiness-Peat and are in a two-class configuration of ten first and 138 economy class seats. As Phoenix is situated in the Arizona desert the airline uses the rather appropriate callsign 'CACTUS'. Photographed at its home base, Phoenix Sky Harbor airport, is A320-200 N625AW. *(Robbie Shaw)*

ANSETT AUSTRALIA (AN/AAA)

Ansett Airways was founded in 1936 and is a well established name in antipodean aviation. With the recent acquisition of Australian Airlines by Qantas, Ansett remains the only major competitor to the national carrier. Its network covers the whole of Australia with the assistance of a number of commuter airlines such as Aeropelican, Flight West, Kendall and Skywest. East West Airlines and its fleet of BAe146s is a recent acquisition. Ansett's sizeable fleet comprises Fokker 28s and 50s, Airbus A320-200s, Boeing 727s, 737s and 767s. The airline has recently acquired two Boeing 747-300s for use on its first international services to Hong Kong and Osaka, although one of

these aircraft suffered damage when a nosewheel collapsed whilst landing at Sydney in October 1994. The Ansett livery features an all-white fuselage with dark blue titling. The dark blue tail is adorned with six white stars of the Southern Cross and a Union flag at the top of the fin. However, the airline has recently adopted a new livery which, at the time of writing, is applied to the 747s. Ansett has twelve A320s with fifteen more on order. Illustrated at Sydney's Kingsford-Smith airport is VH-HYL. The ICAO callsign is 'ANSETT'.

(Robbie Shaw)

BALKAN BULGARIAN AIRLINES (LZ/LAZ)

The Bulgarian national carrier was formed with Soviet assistance in 1945 and, until 1968, operated under the name TABSO. The airline has an extensive route network in Europe, and is also well established in Africa and the Middle East. Like the carriers of most nations under the Soviet sphere of influence it operated predominantly Russian-built equipment, and the Tupolev Tu-154 is still the backbone of the airline's fleet. Balkan was one of the first East European airlines to acquire western equipment with the delivery of the first of three Boeing 737-500s in 1990. The following year the first of four Airbus A320s was taken on charge. Long-haul routes, including a New York service, are operated by a pair of Boeing 767-200ER aircraft leased from Air France. The current livery, which was adopted in 1985, features an all-white fuselage with red and green stripes running most of the length of the fuselage. The same stripes run vertically up the white fin with red titling on the white fuselage, in English on the starboard side and Slavic on the port. Photographed on final approach to Heathrow is the airline's first A320-200 LZ-ABA *Vitosha*. The ICAO callsign is 'BALKAN'.

(Robbie Shaw)

BRANIFF AIRWAYS

Braniff International Airways was one of the most famous names in American aviation circles, perhaps best remembered for the bright and outlandish liveries applied to its aircraft during the 1970s. The airline was formed in 1930 by the brothers Paul and Tom Braniff, and over the following two decades expanded by the acquisition of several carriers. The first international route to Lima was inaugurated in 1948. The first jet to enter service with the company was the Boeing 707, in December 1959. The airline was one of the first customers for the BAC111, a type which it placed in service in 1965. Over the years other jets in the shape of the Boeing 727, 747 and DC-8 entered service with the airline, and the latter type received some outstanding paint schemes. The airline suffered severe financial problems and ceased operations in 1983. The following year a leaner Braniff emerged with support from the Hyatt Corporation and concentrated on a smaller domestic network. The airline became an Airbus customer when it took over Pan American's order for fifty A320s. Sixteen of these were delivered before the airline ceased operations for a second time on 6 November 1989. The airline's A320s wore a livery of a white upper fuselage with bold titling, whilst the colour scheme on the lower fuselage varied between aircraft. Illustrated in desert storage after the airline ceased operations is A320-200 N903BN. This aircraft features a blue lower fuselage. *(Robbie Shaw)*

BRITISH AIRWAYS (BA/BAW)

There are those who say that the letters BA do not stand for British Airways, but Boeing Always. It certainly is true that it is rare to see a non-Boeing aircraft in British Airways livery, although the airline does operate a small number of Concorde and DC-10 aircraft. The latter, however, were inherited when the airline took over British Caledonian, which is why BA presently operates the ten Airbus A320s as they were on order for the independent airline. British Airways' A320 fleet comprises five each of the series -100 and -200, and the airline is one of only three which operates the series -100. The remainder of the BA fleet comprises large numbers of all Boeing products currently in production: the 737, 747, 757 and 767, whilst the new 777 is on order. Over the years Airbus has proved beyond doubt that it produces excellent products, so why BA rebuffs them remains a mystery. Indeed it is understood that the airline would like to dispose of the aircraft, were it not for their popularity with passengers! The British Airways livery comprises a midnight blue lower fuselage and belly with a red 'speedwing' running the entire length of the aircraft. The upper fuselage is pearl grey with midnight blue titling. The top half of the fin is midnight blue, within which is the airline's coat of arms in silver. The lower half of the fin is pearl grey with a quartered Union flag. The airline's A320s are named after British islands, with *Isle of Anglesey* allocated to A320-100 G-BUSC, seen here on approach to Heathrow. The ICAO callsign is 'SPEEDBIRD'. *(Robbie Shaw)*

BRITISH MEDITERRANEAN AIRWAYS (KJ/LAJ)

British Mediterranean Airways is a new airline which commenced operations in the latter part of 1994 with a single A320-200. The airline operates five times a week from London/Heathrow to Beirut, a city somewhat starved of international air services over the past decade. Being a new carrier British Mediterranean managed to obtain precious slots at the London airport, though when the company announced its intentions British Airways promptly applied for the same slots. The regulatory authorities, however, have limited British Airways initially to two flights a week to allow the new airline to establish itself. Like many A320 operators British Mediterranean favours a predominantly white fuselage for its livery, though the belly is dark blue. At the rear of the fuselage the dark blue sweeps up to cover most of the fin, and is emblazoned by a circle of yellow stars – the logo of the European Union. The leading edge of the fin and lower half of the rudder are white, with a diagonal red stripe on the latter. These tail markings are repeated on the white engine cowlings and winglets. Photographed inbound to Heathrow is the sole A320 appropriately registered G-MEDA. The ICAO callsign is 'BMED'. *(SPA Photography)*

CALEDONIAN AIRWAYS (CKT)

When British Airways took over British Caledonian in 1988 it was feared that the famous golden lion logo would be lost for ever. Fortunately that was not the case, as Caledonian Airways was formed to take over the operations of the BA subsidiary British Airtours. The airline's Lockheed Tristars and Boeing 757s operate throughout Europe as well as to the Far East and Caribbean. Two DC-10s are also utilised, and have recently commenced some scheduled services to the Caribbean on behalf of British Airways using BA flight numbers. Early in 1995 it was announced that British Airways had sold Caledonian Airways to the Inspirations Travel Group. This means that at the end of the 1995 summer season the Boeing 757s and probably one of the DC-10s will be returned to BA, from whom they are leased. The company is likely to be in the market for additional DC-10s, and in the meantime during April 1995 took delivery of three Airbus A320s for use on European routes. Initially these will be operated only from UK regional airports rather than the company's Gatwick base. The Caledonian livery consists of a dark blue lower fuselage and engine cowlings, white upper fuselage with dark blue titling and golden yellow pinstripe below the window line. The dark blue fin contains the prominent golden yellow lion rampant. The ICAO callsign is 'CALEDONIAN'. Illustrated is A320-200 G-BUYC. *(Caledonian Airways)*

CANADA 3000 (2T/CMM)

Formed in 1988 as Air 2000 (Canada), the company was soon forced by law to change its name, and decided on the title Canada 3000 Airlines. Based at Toronto the airline operates charter flights to Europe, the USA, the Caribbean and Mexico using a fleet of four Boeing 757s, supplemented by three recently delivered A320s. The latter are used primarily on recently awarded trans-Canada schedules which are extremely popular and invariably full, as the fares are considerably cheaper than the ridiculously high fares charged by the country's two major airlines. During the summer months Europe is the main destination, particularly the UK and France. The winter months, however, are the company's busiest period, as Canadians flee the bitter winter to soak up the Florida, Caribbean and Mexican sunshine. Due to these seasonal fluctuations in traffic levels, Canada 3000 has an agreement with Air 2000 whereby one or two aircraft and crews are swapped between the two carriers to provide additional capacity during each company's busiest periods. This is made easy because the Canada 3000 livery is identical to that of Air 2000, so only the titling has to be changed during such periods. The airline's ICAO callsign is 'ELITE'. Photographed at its Toronto base is A320-200 C-GVXC.

(Robbie Shaw)

CANADIAN AIRLINES INTERNATIONAL (CP/CDN)

Canadian Airlines International is the result of a merger between Canadian Pacific and Pacific Western, two of Canada's independent carriers. Since that merger the airline has also taken over Wardair, one of Canada's aviation legends. Canadian now provides serious competition to Air Canada in both the domestic and international arenas, with an extensive international network stretching across Europe, South America, Asia and Australasia. Within Canada commuter aircraft are operated under the Canadian Regional banner. The company, like many of its US rivals, has recently gone through a tough period financially which forced it to slow down and revise its deliveries of Airbus A320s. A large fleet of Boeing 737-200s remains in use, with Boeing 767-300ERs, DC-10s and three Boeing

747-400s used on international services. The attractive airline livery has the aircraft's belly and engines in deep blue, with a thin red and grey cheatline below the window line leading to the off-white fuselage. The company logo of a large red arrowhead and four deep blue pinstripes on a grey background occupies the centre of the fin, the remainder of which is deep blue. The logo in reduced size is rather cleverly included in the titling on the upper fuselage – CANADIꞱN – thereby avoiding the issue of whether to use the English or French spelling. Photographed being towed from the maintenance hangars at Toronto is A320-200 C-FLSF. The ICAO callsign is 'CANADIAN'. *(Robbie Shaw)*

CHINA AIRLINES (CI/CAL)

China Airlines is the national carrier of the Republic of China or, as it is better known, Taiwan. The airline was formed in 1962 with a piston-engined fleet of Douglas DC-3s and DC-4s and Curtiss C-46s. In 1967 the first jets were introduced in the shape of the Boeing 727, which was soon followed by the 707. A few 737s are used on domestic routes, whilst a number of 747 variants are used on intercontinental and high-density regional routes. The bulk of regional services is undertaken by Airbus A300s, and two Boeing 767s which were also acquired for this purpose were disposed of in favour of further A300s. The most recent acquisition is two leased Airbus A320-200s which were delivered in December 1994 for use on regional routes from Kaohsiung. China Airlines' livery has been unchanged for many years, and comprises a red/white/blue cheatline with the same colours running vertically up the white fin. Lower surfaces are grey, and on the white upper surface is blue titling in both English and Chinese. The ICAO callsign is 'DYNASTY'. Photographed at Bangkok's Don Muang airport is A320-200 3B-RGZ. *(Robbie Shaw)*

CONAIR (KC/OYC)

Founded in 1963 Conair is a major Danish charter operator, with the emphasis on inclusive tour flights to the Canary Islands and holiday destinations around the Mediterranean. Initial operations were undertaken by Douglas DC-7s, which were eventually replaced by Boeing 720s. The airline received more modern equipment in 1987 when it took delivery of the first of three Airbus A300B4s, which were followed by six A320-200s during 1991. Towards the end of 1993 Conair merged with Swedish charter airline Scanair to form Premiair, and the airline's A320s were quickly painted in the new company's livery. The Conair livery comprised a white fuselage bisected by a triple cheatline of three different shades of blue – royal, dark and light, the latter being uppermost. The light blue gradually swept upwards to encompass the fin, upon which was the company's black 'C' logo embracing a golden sun. Illustrated is the airline's final A320-200 OY-CNI *Spica*.

CRETAN AIRLINES (C5/KRT)

Formed during 1991, Cretan Airlines commenced operations during 1993 with three A320-200s leased from troubled Adria Airways. The company is primarily operating in charter services to convey tourists from northern Europe to the Greek islands, particularly Crete. The airline is based at the island's Heraklion airport, and the bulk of flights are operated to Germany. The company has two Dornier Do 328s on order for 1995 delivery with the intention of operating inter-island services – should the Greek government permit it to compete with state-owned Olympic, which is normally protected from such competition. The airline's A320 inventory has been reduced to one, as the other two aircraft were returned to Adria in late 1994. Cretan's livery is based on a white fuselage interrupted only by pale blue tilting and Greek and European Union flags. On the white tail are stylised letters 'CA' in red and blue respectively. Photographed on a regular visit to Frankfurt is A320-200 SX-BAS *Minos*. The ICAO callsign is 'CRETAN'. *(Robbie Shaw)*

CYPRUS AIRWAYS (CY/CYP)

The national airline of Cyprus has expanded considerably since it was formed in 1947 with the assistance of British European Airways. Airbus products predominate in the airline's inventory, though three elderly BAC111s are still in use on regional services. The expanding network covers most of the Middle East and many northern European destinations. In addition to its scheduled services the company operates a number of charter flights throughout the year, particularly from the UK. The A320 is now the backbone of the fleet, though three of the airline's eight aircraft are leased to subsidiary Eurocypria. Supporting the 'minibuses' are four A310-200 wide-bodies, which operate most flights to London's Gatwick and Heathrow airports. Early in the 1990s the company's old livery was superseded and featured a below the window cheatline of orange bordered by white. Above and below were royal blue stripes which widened as they progressed rearwards. The upper stripe curved upwards to cover the whole fin upon which was the company logo, the caricature of a white-winged mountain goat. Photographed on the runway at Luton is A320-200 5B-DAU. The ICAO callsign is 'CYPRUS'. *(Robbie Shaw)*

During 1991 most of the Cyprus Airways fleet received the new livery which retained the original blue and gold colours, signifying sea and sand. The engines and lower fuselage are grey and are separated from the white upper fuselage by a triple cheatline of gold, white and royal blue. The dark blue titling and national flag appear on the cabin roof. On the white fin are the blue and gold colours in the shape of a fin, and upon the lower blue portion is the white-winged mountain goat logo. Illustrated wearing the new livery on final approach to Athens is A320-200 5B-DAU named *Evelthon*. *(Robbie Shaw)*

DRAGONAIR (KA/HDA)

Dragonair, or, as it is officially titled, Hong Kong Dragon Airlines, was formed in 1985 with a single Boeing 737-200 as a charter operator. A second 737 followed and, as the airline built up its network of scheduled charter destinations, the 737 fleet rose to five. Dragonair achieved its aim of scheduled carrier status, and soon afterwards the Swire Group, Cathay Pacific's parent company, became a major investor in the airline. Dragonair's extensive network of Chinese services was extended when Cathay transferred its Beijing and Shanghai services to be operated by two Tristars which it leased to the smaller airline. In December 1991 Dragonair announced that it was to replace its 737 fleet and the aircraft chosen was the Airbus A320-200, seven of which are leased from the International Lease Finance Corporation. The first was

delivered in January 1993 and the seventh in mid-1994, and these, supported by the two Tristars, operate to twenty-three destinations in seven countries. Dragonair has an option in which it can trade its A320s for the larger A321, and during 1995, it will take delivery of two leased A330s. With the acquisition of the Airbus products the airline took the opportunity to introduce a new livery. This is based on an all-white scheme broken only by the bold titling in both English and Chinese characters on the forward fuselage. The airline's dragon logo appears in red on the fin, and is repeated on a smaller scale on the engine cowlings. The officially allocated ICAO callsign is 'LOONGAIR' but 'DRAGONAIR' is actually used. Illustrated at Hong Kong's Kai Tak airport is A320-200 VR-HYU.
(Robbie Shaw)

EGYPTAIR (MS/MSR)

Egyptair is one of the oldest airlines in the Middle East, though it has only been known by its present title since 1971. When formed at Cairo in 1932 it operated under the title Misrair Airwork, then becoming just Misrair, then United Arab Airlines. When services to Europe commenced British aircraft in the shape of Viscounts and Comet 4Cs were used; however, during the close association with the USSR a number of Soviet types were acquired. These included An-24s, Il-18s and Il-62s, and Tu-154s, though a number of 707s and 737s were acquired from Boeing. The Soviet equipment has since been disposed of in favour of an all-western fleet. The inventory now comprises solely Boeing and Airbus types. The latter includes fourteen A300s and seven A320-200s. The colour scheme has a white fuselage with a broad red cheatline, underneath which is a thinner gold band. Both colours run up the white fin where they are interrupted by a gold disc containing the company logo – the head of Horus, a falcon-headed god of ancient Egypt, in a vivid red and black. The red titling on the cabin roof is in both English and Arabic. Awaiting take-off clearance from London/Heathrow is A320-200 SU-GBF which is named after the town of Sharm El Sheikh. The ICAO callsign is 'EGYPTAIR'. *(Robbie Shaw)*

EUROCYPRIA AIRLINES (UI/ECA)

A subsidiary of Cyprus Airways, Eurocypria was founded in 1990. Using three of the parent company's Airbus A320-200s the company operates inclusive tour charter flights bringing residents of northern Europe to sunny Cyprus. The climate on the island ensures that there are tourists all year round, and Eurocypria has a major market in conveying passengers from the UK's regional airports. Eurocypria's livery is not unlike that of its parent company. It features grey engines and lower fuselage and a white upper fuselage, upon which is the blue titling and national flag. The cheatline features below the window line dark and light blue bands interspersed by white bands. On the white fin is a gold circle and wavy blue line, no doubt representing sun and sand. Photographed on a crisp December day at Edinburgh's Turnhouse airport is A320-200 5B-DBB *Akamas*. The ICAO callsign is 'EUROCYPRIA'.

(Robbie Shaw)

EXCALIBUR AIRWAYS (EXC)

Excalibur Airways was formed on 1 May 1992 when it acquired the assets of Trans European Airways (UK), which ceased operations towards the end of 1991. Although based at East Midlands, the bulk of the airline's operations are undertaken from London/Gatwick using a fleet of four Airbus A320-200s leased from Guiness-Peat. All four aircraft were acquired in 1992, and the airline's fleet was kept extremely busy during the 1994 summer season, so much so that a Boeing 737-300 was leased for that period. The airline operates charter flights to a number of destinations in the Mediterranean area, and is particularly strong on Egyptian and Israeli routes. The aircraft are operated in a 180-seat one-class configuration. The livery has an all-white fuselage with tilting just above the window line. The tail is purple, and emblazoned upon it is the bold logo of the hilt of a silver sword. The airline's four aircraft carry personalized out of sequence registrations, such as G-KMAM illustrated here. This particular aircraft was the 301st A320 built. The ICAO callsign is 'EXCALIBUR'. *(Robbie Shaw)*

FLITESTAR

South African carrier Flitestar ceased operations in the first quarter of 1994, unable to sustain losses while making a determined bid to compete on the domestic market with national carrier South African Airlines. The company was attracting increasing numbers of passengers, and shortly before its demise announced its intention of starting international services from its Johannesburg base to London/Gatwick. The airline can trace its history back to 1953 when it was known as Trek Airways, changing to the Flitestar title in October 1991. When it ceased operations the airline had a fleet of two ATR-72s and four A320-200s, with all of the latter leased from Guiness-Peat. The airline's livery was similar in style to that of Excalibur, featuring an all-white fuselage apart from the titling. The tail was royal blue with a large white star emblazoned on it. Seen as it rotates from the runway is A320-200, ZS-NZR. *(Airbus Industrie)*

GULF AIR (GF/GFA)

Gulf Air was set up as the national carrier for the Arabian (Persian) Gulf states of Bahrain, Oman, Qatar and the United Arab Emirates; however, in 1985 the latter country set up its own carrier, Emirates Airlines. Gulf Air can trace its history to 1950 when it was formed as Gulf Aviation to operate regional services from Bahrain with an Avro Anson, which was later replaced by DH Doves, Herons and Douglas DC-3s. The first jet equipment was the BAC 111 followed by VC-10s leased from the then BOAC. From 1986 Lockheed L1011 Tristars operated the bulk of international services, and a small number of these aircraft are still in use. Backbone of the fleet is now the Boeing 767-300ER, twenty of which are in use. These are being sup-plemented by six Airbus A340s which are in the process of delivery, and whose range has permitted the carrier to start a Bahrain–New York direct service. Twelve A320-200s are now in use on regional services, superseding Boeing 737-200s. Gulf Air's livery comprises a white fuselage with three bands in purple, green and red from the nose to the wing root, gradually thinning as they proceed aft. The same colours cover the top half of the fin, this time in vertical format. The lower fin is white with a golden falcon superimposed, whilst gold tilting in English and Arabic is on the upper fuselage. This pleasing shot shows A320-200 A40-EH. The ICAO callsign is 'GULF AIR'. *(Airbus Industrie)*

IBERIA (IB/IBE)

At the time of writing, Iberia, Spain's national carrier, is going through a survival crisis. In an effort to stem mounting losses the airline announced swingeing cuts on staff and salaries, the result of which was a series of damaging strikes by the unhappy work force which merely compounded the airline's troubles. It now appears that an accord has been reached and the airline has announced a number of cost-saving measures. Holdings in a number of airlines such as Aerolineas Argentinas, Aviaco, Binter Canarias, Ladeco and Viasa will be sold to raise cash, as will the holding in a ground-handling subsidiary. The airline's network will contract considerably to become a regional rather than global carrier. An agreement has been reached whereby 757s being delivered will be leased rather than bought, A321s and A340s on order have been cancelled, and A300s which were in store have been brought back into service. Iberia has a fleet of twenty-two A320-200s, the first of which was delivered in December 1990. The bright livery features the national colours in the form of a triple cheatline of red, orange and yellow which runs the length of the white fuselage, sweeping up above and behind the cockpit. The white tail contains a stylised 'IB', the letters in red and yellow respectively. Within the dot of the 'I' is a gold crown signifying the Spanish monarchy. Photographed about to land at London/Heathrow is A320-200 EC-FLQ *Dunas de Liencres*. The ICAO callsign is 'IBERIA'. *(Robbie Shaw)*

INDIAN AIRLINES (IC/IAC)

Indian Airlines is the country's main domestic carrier which, in recent years, has expanded services to include destinations in neighbouring Asian countries and the Middle East. The airline has in use a fleet of over sixty jet aircraft of three different types. Some twenty of these are elderly Boeing 737-200s, the first of which was delivered in 1970. Numerically the A320 is the most important, with twenty-six in use and a further four on order. These are supplemented by eleven A300s which are used primarily on high-density domestic routes between the major cities – Bombay, Calcutta and Delhi. The airline became the first to lose an A320 on a revenue service when VT-EPN crashed short of the runway at Bangalore on 14 February 1990. Immediately after this the airline grounded its A320s for a short period, an act which was not followed by any other A320 operator. Indian Airlines' rather plain livery comprises a white fuselage with a grey belly. Black titling above the window line is in English on one side and Hindi on the other. The whole tail fin is orange upon which are the stylised letters 'IA' in white. Photographed at Bangkok inbound from Calcutta is A320-200 VT-EPD. The ICAO callsign is 'INDAIR'. *(Robbie Shaw)*

INTER EUROPEAN AIRWAYS

Inter European Airways was a Cardiff-based operator which was formed in 1986 as a subsidiary of Aspro Holidays, and commenced operations in 1987 with leased Boeing 737-200s. These were replaced the following year by series -300 aircraft and a few Boeing 757s. The bulk of the airline's operations were from Cardiff and Bristol to a variety of European holiday destinations. Early in 1993 the airline expanded further with the acquisition of two Airbus A320-200s; however, by that autumn it had ceased to exist as parent company Aspro was taken over by Airtours International. The A320s and 757s were quickly repainted into Airtours livery but the 737s were returned to the lessor. Inter European's livery featured two pairs of 'candy' striped cheatlines along the lower fuselage in red, yellow and white which swept up the trailing edge of the white fin, which contained the stylised initials IEA. The upper fuselage was white with black titles and the belly of the aircraft was brown. The fuselage stripes were repeated on the engine cowlings. Illustrated on the ramp at Salzburg is A320-200 G-IEAF. *(Kajetan Steiner)*

KUWAIT AIRWAYS (KU/KAC)

Kuwait Airways is the national carrier of this small but rich Arab state. The airline has had to rebuild much of its infrastructure and partially re-equip following the invasion by Iraq and the subsequent Gulf War. The invading Iraqis stole much of the airline's equipment as well as some of its aircraft, notably Airbuses, two Boeing 767s, a 727 and some executive jets. Some of these aircraft have eventually been recovered and refurbished. Newly delivered are three Airbus A320s which support A300s and A310s on regional and international routes. Intercontinental services are still undertaken by the four Boeing 747-200s, though three series -400s are due for delivery commencing in August 1995. The two Boeing 767s have still to be returned but the third aircraft is currently leased out. The recently modified livery features a predominantly white fuselage interrupted by a thin blue cheatline bordered by a lower black pinstripe which runs the length of the fuselage below the window line. Apart from the extreme top and bottom, the tail fin is blue, within which is the airline's white stylised bird logo. Black titling is on the lower fin and upper fuselage. Illustrated wearing its pre-delivery registration is the airline's third A320-200, 9K-AKC *Qurtoba*. The ICAO callsign is 'KUWAIT'. *(Author's collection)*

LACSA (LR/LRC)

LACSA – Lineas Aereas de Costa Rica SA – is the national carrier of the small Central American nation and operates from the capital San José. The airline was formed in 1945 by Pan American and the Costa Rican government using a fleet of DC-3s. The airline's network encompasses much of Central America, as well as destinations in Mexico and Venezuela. The company also serves the US destinations of Los Angeles, Miami, New Orleans and New York. The elderly fleet of Boeing 727s has all but been disposed of in favour of 737-200s while five new A320-200s are leased from GATX. These operate the bulk of the US services. The airline's livery is based on the red, white and blue of the national flag. Pinstripes of these colours run the length of the white fuselage below the window line, broken only by the bold titling forward of the wing root. The pinstripes sweep up to encompass the whole fin, widening as they do so. Illustrated on the runway at Miami is A320-200 N481GX. The ICAO callsign is 'LACSA'. *(Author's collection)*

LEISURE AIR (L8/LWD)

Leisure Air is the airline operating on behalf of Worldwide Aviation Services and, although the latter has its headquarters in Washington DC, Leisure Air's main operating base is Winston-Salem, North Carolina. The airline was set up in 1992 to tap the vast American leisure and vacation market, which included transporting holiday-makers from the northern states to destinations such as Las Vegas. Three A320s were acquired in the autumn of 1992 with a further two following a year later. These were supported by two second-hand Boeing 757s and a similar number of DC-10-10s. During the summer of 1994 the company inaugurated a weekly San Francisco–London/Stansted service with a DC-10-30. Recently, however, the airline has fallen foul of the US Federal Aviation Administration over maintenance practices and has had its operating certificate revoked.

The authorities then permitted the airline to recommence operations, but only with the A320s. However, the resurrection was short-lived and the company has just ceased operations. The livery primarily featured two colours, dark blue and white. The dividing line is wing root level, above which is white, with dark blue titling and three stars on the cabin roof. The dark blue sweeps upwards to cover all of the rear fuselage and most of the tail, with the extreme top and leading edge being white. Within the dark blue portion of the tail are the stylised letters 'LA', while a red band runs from underneath the nose along the window line, and vertically up the fin. Illustrated is A320-200 N317RX. The ICAO callsign is 'LEISURE WORLD'. *(Author's collection)*

LUFTHANSA (LH/DLH)

Lufthansa began jet operations in 1960 with the introduction of the Boeing 707, which was soon followed by the smaller Boeing 720. The airline was the first in Europe to receive the Boeing 727 and was a launch customer for the successful 737, a type which still dominates the airline's short-haul fleet. Not surprisingly Lufthansa has also operated the 747 Jumbo in significant numbers. Despite being a strong supporter of Boeing products the German carrier was quick to recognise the quality of Airbus products, and its inventory currently comprises Airbus A300s, A310s, A320s, A321s and A340s; indeed, only the A330 has escaped the clutches of Lufthansa's pilots.

The airline was an early customer for the A320, the first being delivered in October 1989. It has thirty-three series -200s, all of which are in a two-class 144-seat configuration. The current livery was unveiled in 1988 and features a white fuselage from the wing root upwards; the lower fuselage is grey. Bold dark blue titling is on the cabin roof, whilst on the dark blue tail is the company logo of a stylised flying crane within a yellow circle. Lufthansa's A320s are named after German towns, such as *Troisdorf*, which is allocated to D-AIPM. The ICAO callsign is 'LUFTHANSA'. *(Robbie Shaw)*

MEXICANA (MX/MXA)

Mexicana has recently undergone a reorganisation, and although a large number of Boeing 727s are in use they are now complemented by Airbus A320s. There are presently sixteen A320s in use, six of which are leased, whilst orders and options account for a further eight and fourteen respectively. The Airbus products are being increasingly used to the many US destinations, supplemented by five ageing DC-10s. The company has an extensive domestic network, and is assisted by four commuter airlines which feed traffic to the main hubs. The airline has a long history dating back to 1921 when it was founded as Compania Mexicana de Transportes Aereos, adopting its current name three years later. With the introduction of the A320s the company took the opportunity to introduce a major revision of its livery. This is now based on a white fuselage with titles below the window line. At the rear of the fuselage a pastel shade proceeds upwards to encompass the whole fin, and upon the pastel shade is a series of leaf-type patterns. Perhaps with photographers in mind, the airline applied a number of different shades, including yellow, amber and green. However, it would appear that this was becoming difficult and perhaps expensive to maintain, and the company is going to standardise on one colour. In the centre of the fin is a white stylised 'A' Aztec logo. Illustrated is leased A320-200 N225RX, named *Atlixcayoti*. The ICAO callsign is 'MEXICANA'. *(Airbus Industrie)*

Featuring yet another of Mexicana's innovative schemes is A320-200
XA-RYT *Zapoteco* inbound to land on runway 25L at Los Angeles.
(Robbie Shaw)

MONARCH AIRLINES (ZB/MON)

A long-established and well known name in the holiday charter market is Luton-based Monarch Airlines. The company was formed in 1967, initially using Bristol Britannias and Boeing 720s, to carry customers for its parent company Cosmos. In recent years the company has seen a steady expansion of its fleet which comprises Boeing 737s, 757s and Airbus A300s and A320s, the latter being the most recent acquisitions. The A300s and Boeing 757s are used on both long- and short-haul routes. The livery features an all-white fuselage with yellow (upper) and black (lower) cheatlines with black titling on the upper fuselage. The company's black crowned 'M' logo is located on the white fin whilst the belly and engine nacelles are grey. Monarch operates its A320 in a one-class 179-seat configuration, and the first of the airline's seven A320-200s was delivered in January 1993. That aircraft, G-MONY, formerly served with Canadian Airlines International as C-FLSF and is illustrated here. The ICAO callsign is 'MONARCH'. *(Robbie Shaw)*

NORTHWEST AIRLINES (NW/NWA)

Northwest Airlines is one of America's largest and oldest carriers. It was formed in 1934 and expansion took in a number of destinations in the Pacific and Far East; hence, until 1985 it was known as Northwest Orient. The airline has since expanded eastwards across the Atlantic and now serves destinations in the UK, Eire, Germany, Scandinavia and the Netherlands. The airline has a major marketing and code share agreement with KLM. The airline operates a large fleet of elderly DC-9s of many variants and, despite the delivery of fifty A320s, a number of the DC-9s are to be retained and fitted with hush-kitted engines. Northwest also operates substantial numbers of Boeing 727s and 757s. It was also the launch customer for the 747-400, which it operates alongside older series -100s and -200s. The current livery was introduced in 1991, and is a significant improvement on the old scheme. The cabin roof and tail fin are bright red, and at the top of the latter is the company stylised 'N' logo within a white circle. The white titling is within the broad grey cheatline, below which is a thin dark blue stripe which broadens at the rear of the fuselage. The belly and engine cowlings are white. Photographed on final approach to Detroit/Metropolitan airport is A320-200 N326US. The ICAO callsign is 'NORTHWEST'.

ONUR AIR (8Q/OHY)

Turkey is a country which seems to produce countless charter operators which seem to last only a few years before disappearing into obscurity. One of the latest start-ups is Istanbul-based Onur Air which, unlike most of its predecessors, has forsaken geriatric jets such as the Boeing 727 and Tupolev Tu-154 and opted for new-build Airbus A320s. The airline was formed in 1992 and appears to be doing well in the holiday charter market. It currently operates five A320-200s leased from two different sources. Like most Turkish charter outfits the bulk of traffic originates in Germany, though its aircraft can be seen at many other airports in northern Europe. The colour scheme is dominated by the white fuselage favoured by A320 operators, with thin red and black pinstripes running the length of the aircraft below the window line. Dark blue titling and the Turkish flag appear on the cabin roof, whilst on the white tail is the logo of red and black rings, within which is a red 'speedwing'-type motif. Illustrated is the airline's first A320, TC-ONA *Birtug*. The ICAO callsign is 'ONUR AIR'. *(Robbie Shaw)*

PEGASUS AIRLINES (PGT)

Pegasus Airlines, founded in 1990, is yet another Turkish charter airline. It is a subsidiary of Aer Lingus and operates three Boeing 737-400s on charters from northern Europe to a number of Turkish destinations, principally the airports serving the main holiday resorts. During the summer of 1993, to make up for a shortage of capacity, the airline leased an A320 from Adria Airways, though this aircraft was flown in an anonymous all-white livery. With the exception of the tail logo the normal Pegasus livery is identical to that of another Aer Lingus subsidiary, Futura Airlines of Spain. This features a white fuselage with red and yellow cheatlines running below the window line. Before reaching the cockpit these lines curve downwards underneath the forward fuselage where the yellow broadens significantly. Towards the rear of the fuselage the yellow band sweeps upward and broadens to cover the whole fin, upon which is the white logo of Pegasus – a winged horse. The A320 mentioned, S5-AAC, is seen on push-back at a rather wet Düsseldorf in September 1993. The ICAO callsign is 'PEGASUS'.
(Robbie Shaw)

PREMIAIR (DK/VKG)

Premiair is Scandinavia's largest charter operator and was formed towards the end of 1993 with the merger of Denmark's Conair and Sweden's Scanair. Very quickly all six of Conair's A320s and Scanair's four DC-10s were painted in the livery of the new company. This is based on an all-white scheme broken only by the tail logo of a large orange disc superimposed over a blue disc, and black titling on the cabin roof and engine cowlings. The airline's market is conveying Scandinavian tourists to the warmer climates of the Mediterranean and the Canary Islands. The latter is probably the airline's main destination, and I have seen as many as five A320s and three DC-10s at Las Palmas in the space of a few hours! Photographed on its take-off roll from Las Palmas is A320-200 OY-CNG. The rather appropriate ICAO callsign is 'VIKING'.

(Robbie Shaw)

ROYAL JORDANIAN AIRLINES (RJ/RJA)

Formed in 1963 as Alia–Royal Jordanian Airlines, the company was designated the national carrier to replace Jordanian Airways. Initial equipment comprised two Handley-Page Heralds and a single DC-7, with the Sud-Aviation Caravelle joining the inventory in 1965. These were supplemented and eventually replaced by the Boeing 727, while the 707 and 720 variants were purchased in 1971 for long-haul routes. Alia was the first of the Arab national carriers to commence scheduled services to the USA and acquired a pair of Boeing 747s for the route, but these have since been disposed of. Largest type in the inventory is the Lockheed L1011 Tristar which operates most intercontinental and some European services. These are supported by Airbus A310s, while two A320s are used on regional routes. The airline has a third A320 which is currently surplus to requirements and is stored, though it still has options on a further three. In 1986 the airline unveiled a dramatic new colour scheme and name, being known simply as Royal Jordanian. The lower white fuselage is sharply contrasted by the dark charcoal grey which envelops the rest of the aircraft, including the fin. On the charcoal just below the window line is a gold cheatline bordered by an upper red pinstripe, and on the cabin roof is the gold airline titling in both English and Arabic. The tail contains a large Hashemite crown in bright gold whilst black tapered speed bands run horizontally up the fin, which is topped by a red band. Illustrated is an A320-200 on a pre-delivery test flight. The ICAO callsign is 'JORDANIAN'. *(Airbus Industrie)*

SAETA (EH/SET)

The letters SAETA stand for Sociedad Ecuatoriana de Transportes Aereos. The airline was formed towards the end of 1966 with a single Piper Aztec. Jet equipment arrived in 1981 in the shape of a single Boeing 727, which was soon followed by a 707. In recent years the company has expanded its network further, particularly since the demise of the national carrier Ecuatoriana. From its base at Quito the company operates domestic services to Guayaquil and regional services to Bogota, Buenos Aires, Caracas, Lima, Mexico City and Santiago. In the US, Los Angeles, Miami and New York are also served. Two Boeing 727s and a single 737 are operated, whilst more modern equipment in the shape of two Airbus A310s and a single A320 has recently been added to the inventory. The company livery used to be blue and white, but the A320 features the almost obligatory white fuselage with large dark blue titles forward of the wing root. The rear fuselage and tail fin are bright red, upon which is a white arrowhead. The latter colours are repeated on the winglets, while the engine cowlings are grey. On the port side of the aircraft LAPSA Air Paraguay titles are displayed instead of those of SAETA. A consortium led by SAETA owns 80 per cent of LAPSA. The aircraft in question, HC-BTV, is illustrated here. The ICAO callsign is 'SAETA'. *(Author's collection)*

SHOROUK AIR (7Q/SHK)

A newcomer to the aviation scene is Cairo-based Shorouk Air which was formed in 1992. The airline is a joint venture company between Egyptair and Kuwait Airways, and operates both scheduled and charter services. Scheduled destinations include Beirut, Cairo, Kuwait and Luxor. Charter services are flown to a number of European destinations where they ferry tourists to Egypt. Initial equipment comprised three Airbus A320-200s, the first two of which were delivered in September 1992. The airline also ordered four Boeing 757s, two of which are the PF package freighter variant. None has yet been delivered and the airline has in fact cancelled two of these aircraft; no doubt the dearth of tourists visiting Egypt due to the continuing terrorist problems is a significant factor. The cheerful livery features orange and blue bands running below the window line on the white fuselage, with these bands repeated on the white engine cowlings. On a royal blue tail fin is an orange and yellow disc, over which are four white horizontal pinstripes. The blue titling on the cabin roof is in both English and Arabic. Photographed at Düsseldorf in October 1992, just weeks after delivery, is the second A320-200 SU-RAB. *(Iain Logan)*

SKYSERVICE (SKL)

Skyservice is a new Canadian charter operator which commenced operations during the winter of 1994/95 with two Airbus A320s leased from Monarch Airlines. Most operations are from Toronto, and like all Canadian charter operators the airline is kept busy during the bitter winters conveying Canadian tourists to the warmer climes of Florida and the Caribbean. The A320s are only on lease until the spring, at which time they will be returned to the UK ready for Monarch's busy summer schedule. Due to the short duration of the lease these aircraft have retained their Monarch cheatline but have red Skyservice titles on the cabin roof. The tail fin has been painted black with a red quartered maple leaf superimposed on the lower half. The ICAO callsign is 'SKYSERVICE'.

(Val Omajnikov via Bob Henderson)

SOUTH AFRICAN AIRWAYS (SA/SAA)

The national airline of the Republic of South Africa is South African Airways (SAA) which was formed in 1934. The airline took over the route and aircraft – three Junkers F13s and one Junkers W4 which had previously been operated by Union Airways, though these aircraft were quickly replaced by Junkers Ju 52s. The acquisition in 1935 of South West African Airways gave South African an extensive network of regional services. At the end of the Second World War a London service was inaugurated initially using Avro Yorks, and later DC-4s. Within a few years the airline was operating Vickers Vikings and Douglas DC-3 and DC-4 aircraft to many destinations throughout Africa. Modernisation saw the introduction of Constellations, Viscounts, DC-7s and Comet 1s, and the expansion of international services to include Australia. The Boeing 707 was acquired for intercontinental routes, followed by both the 727 and 737 for domestic and regional services. Boeing 747's are now used on long-haul routes, including four series -400s. The first Airbus product was delivered in the final months of 1976, and the airline now operates eight A300s and seven A320s. The airline's livery has a dark blue cheatline below the window line, trimmed by lower white and orange stripes. The lower fuselage is grey, the upper white with black titling which is in English on the port side and Afrikaans on the starboard. The bright orange fin shows off the company's logo of a dark blue winged springbok outlined in white. Illustrated is the airline's first A320-200 ZS-SHA named *Blue Crane*. The ICAO callsign is 'SPRINGBOK'. *(Airbus Industrie)*

SOUTHEAST EUROPEAN AIRLINES (6J/GRE)

SEEA – Southeast European Airlines – is a small Greek carrier which was formed in 1990 and began operations with a single Cessna 421. These have since been supplemented by three nineteen-seat SA227 Metroliners and two fifty-seat Fokker 50s. In January 1994 an A320 was taken on charge, being the first of two it intended to lease from ORIX Leasing, though as it happened the second aircraft never materialised. The aircraft was utilised on an Athens–London service in a configuration of twelve business and 138 economy seats. This service was operated as a franchise agreement with Virgin Atlantic, with the aircraft and crews in the livery and uniforms of the British carrier. During the summer of 1994 a further two A320s were acquired from ORIX but operated on behalf of Ambassador Airways, an airline which has since ceased operations, and the aircraft returned to the lessor. Early in 1995 the

A320 which operated the Athens service was repossessed after SEEA allegedly failed to meet leasing payments, and Virgin is now planning the acquisition of an A320 to operate the service itself. As mentioned, the aircraft on the London route was operated in full Virgin livery: a white fuselage interrupted only by the Virgin logo underneath the cockpit, red engines and a red tail – the white titling appears on the latter. The aircraft in question, A320-200 SX-BSV, is seen here taxiing at London's Heathrow airport. The airline used the 'VIRGIN' callsign on the London route, the flight numbers being 1000/1001. When the service first started, however, the flight number was 2000/2001, and the Greek operator used the callsign 'GRECIAN'. It is obvious someone had a sense of humour.

(Robbie Shaw)

SUDAN AIRWAYS (SD/SUD)

Sudan Airways is the national carrier of Sudan with its headquarters and main operating base at Khartoum. The company has sixteen aircraft of six different types on its inventory, which is hardly conducive to economical operations. These include DHC Twin Otters and Fokker 50s, the former being operated for UNICEF and government agencies. Two Boeing 737-200s are operated on regional and domestic routes, supported by elderly Boeing 707s. Airbus Industrie products include a single A320-200 and two A310-300s. The Airbus products are used on services to Europe, namely Frankfurt and London/Heathrow. Sudan Air has recently commenced a London/Gatwick–Khartoum–Johannesburg service,

although this route is operated by a former Hawaiian Air Lockheed L1011 Tristar leased from, and operated by, Air Ops of Sweden. The Sudan Air livery features a white fuselage with a blue/yellow/blue cheatline. This cheatline commences at the nose, but on the forward fuselage sweeps upwards to run above the window line. The tail fin is yellow, apart from the leading edge which is white. The blue titling runs vertically up the forward edge of the fin, in English on the starboard side and Arabic on the port. Photographed as it rotates from the Toulouse runway is Sudan Air's sole A320-200 F-GMAI. This aircraft has since been re-registered F-OKAI. The ICAO callsign is 'SUDANAIR'. *(Airbus Industrie)*

TRANSASIA AIRLINES (GE/TNA)

Foshing Airlines was formed in 1951 as a regional airline of the Republic of China (Taiwan). In recent years the company has undergone a modernisation programme which has seen some seventeen ATR-42s and -72s join the airline's fleet. From its base at Taipei's Sung-Shan airport the company operates to most airports in the country, where air travel is extensively used due to chaotic road traffic conditions. The airline was one of the first Asian carriers to order the Airbus A320. These aircraft never wore Foshing livery, however, as prior to the delivery of the first of the two aircraft in August 1992 the company was renamed TransAsia Airlines. These two machines are operated in an all-economy 162-sear configuration. The company has also ordered four A321s in a 194-seat configuration with deliveries commencing in late 1995. Like that of many A320 operators TransAsia's livery features a white fuselage, broken only by three stripes of orange, green and blue which run over the spine at mid-fuselage level, stopping just above the window line where the titling is in both English and Chinese characters. On the orange tail is a gold disc, within which is a stylised dragon logo. Illustrated is TransAsia's first A320-200 B-22301. *(Airbus Industrie)*

TRANSLIFT AIRWAYS (T7/TLA)

Ireland's Translift Airways was founded in October 1991 and commenced passenger charter flights five months later. The airline built up a fleet of DC-8-71 series aircraft which were used on both passenger and cargo charters, including sub charters on behalf of some European carriers. The company also briefly operated transatlantic scheduled flights from Dublin and Shannon to Los Angeles. These have now been discontinued and the DC-8s have been disposed of; the fleet now comprises four Airbus A320-200s leased from ORIX. These are flown in a 180-seat all-economy configuration used predominantly on tourist charter flights to European holiday resorts. The airline is yet another to favour the all-white fuselage, which features three black and grey pinstripes at wing root level. On the forward fuselage the bold black titling is sandwiched between the pinstripes and window line. On the gloss-black tail is a white ring, within which is a Gaelic-style white 'T'. These colours are repeated on the engine cowlings. Illustrated is the airline's third A320, EI-TLF. Note the European Union logo featuring gold stars on a blue background painted on the winglets. The ICAO callsign is 'TRANSLIFT'. *(Robbie Shaw)*

TUNIS AIR (TU/TAR)

The Tunisian national airline, Tunis Air, was formed in 1948. Services between Tunis, Algiers and Paris commenced with a single DC-3 and, following the acquisition of a DC-4, expansion of the route network embraced Lyon, Marseilles and Rome. As with the airlines of many former French colonies, the Sud-Aviation Caravelle was selected as the airline's first jet equipment. Tunis Air now has an extensive network throughout Europe and the Middle East using Boeing 727s, 737s, A320s and a single A300. The latter is used predominantly on the high-density Paris/Orly–Tunis route. The first A320 was delivered in October 1990 and the company currently has seven A320-200s, with a further five on order. The present colour scheme was introduced to coincide with the introduction of the A320s and is based on an all-white scheme with red titling in both English and Arabic. On the tail is a large leaping gazelle with trailing pinstripes, all in red. Illustrated at Zurich is the airline's first A320, TS-IMC, named *7 Novembre*. The ICAO callsign is 'TUNAIR'. *(Robbie Shaw)*

UNITED AIRLINES (UA/UAL)

United Airlines is one of the largest in the US, and has undergone a steady expansion into Europe since it acquired the routes of the now defunct Pan American. The airline undertook similar expansion in the Pacific and Asia regions in 1986, again at Pan American's expense. United's large fleet of over 400 aircraft consists mainly of Boeing products, with large numbers of the 727, 737, 747, 757 and 767 in the inventory, and as these words are read the airline should have received its first 777. The airline also uses the DC-10 and is in the process of taking delivery of fifty Airbus A320-200s. United introduced a new livery in January 1993, which came as something of surprise, being one of the best kept secrets in commercial aviation. The new livery features a medium-grey upper fuselage with white titling, below which are two thin red and blue pinstripes running below the window line. The engine nacelles and fuselage from the wing root downwards are midnight blue. The tail is covered with black and blue horizontal stripes, upon which is the red and blue 'U'-shaped logo. On 20 January 1995 United took delivery of its twenty-second A320 – the 500th built. Illustrated inbound to Los Angeles is A320-200 N408UA. The ICAO callsign is 'UNITED'. *(Robbie Shaw)*

UNITED EUROPEAN AIRWAYS

United European Airways was the name of a new Turkish charter operator which was founded in 1992. The company ordered three A320s from Kawasaki Leasing, and the aircraft were painted in the airline's attractive livery. However, problems arose and the airline never commenced operations. Illustrated in temporary storage wearing the pre-delivery registration F-WWBJ is one of the A320s intended for United European. *(Author's collection)*

VIETNAM AIRLINES (VN/HVN)

Vietnam has recently emerged from years of isolation, which is good news for the rapidly expanding Vietnam Airlines. The company was formerly known as Hang Khong Vietnam and operated Soviet-built equipment, including Ilyushin Il-18 and Tupolev Tu-134 aircraft. These are still in use but their days are numbered as western jet equipment is acquired. Two Boeing 737-300s were operated by TEA Switzerland on behalf of the Vietnamese national carrier, but have since returned to Europe. The airline is now receiving assistance from Air France, from whom seven A320s are leased. These are used on the majority of the Asian

regional services, supported by three leased Boeing 767s on the higher density routes. With the new equipment a new livery was introduced, featuring a predominantly white fuselage with a blue cheatline, and a further blue band running underneath the forward fuselage and sweeping up to join the cheatline just behind the cockpit. On the white fin is the new logo of a diagonal blue band attached to a blue ring, with a small national flag at the top of the rudder. Illustrated at Hong Kong's Kai Tak airport is A320-200 F-GFKY. The ICAO callsign is 'VIETNAM AIRLINES'.

(Robbie Shaw)

COCKPIT SHOT

The modern cockpit of the A320 looks rather spartan when compared to older types with analogue instrumentation. Note the absence of the traditional yoke or control column. Instead pilots control the aircraft by use of the side-stick. This feature is repeated on other Airbus products such as the A321, A330 and A340.
(Airbus Industrie)